20
COMMUNICATION TIPS
FOR COUPLES

A 30-MINUTE GUIDE TO A BETTER RELATIONSHIP

DOYLE BARNETT

NEW WORLD LIBRARY
NOVATO, CALIFORNIA

New World Library
14 Pamaron Way • Novato, California • 94949

Cover painting: Chagall, Marc. *Birthday [l'Anniversaire]*. (1915)
$31\frac{3}{4}$ x $39\frac{1}{4}$" (80.6 x 99.7 cm). The Museum of Modern Art, New York.
Acquired through the Lillie P. Bliss Bequest.
Photograph © 1995 The Museum of Modern Art, New York.

Cover design: Mary Powers Design, San Francisco

Library of Congress Cataloging-in-Publication Data

Barnett, Doyle, 1956–
Twenty communication tips for couples :
a 30-minute guide to a better relationship / Doyle Barnett.
p.   cm.   ISBN 1-880032-68-6 (pbk.)
1. Communication in marriage.   2. Interpersonal communication.
3. Man-woman relationships.   I. Title.

HQ734.B2495   1995   95-2938
646.7'8 — dc20   CIP

Printed in Canada on acid-free paper
Distributed by Publishers Group West
10 9 8 7

CONTENTS

III

v

FOreWorD

This book is a quick, easy guide to some key communication skills. You can practice them every day, with every person; however, some of these skills are best used with the people you love and trust the most.

I believe that trust is the foundation for loving, fulfilling, and powerful relationships. Despite my work with many couples over the years, I still don't know how to assist a relationship in which one or both partners are not completely honest with each other.

When you know your partner's actions are motivated more by their concern for you and your needs than they are by their own needs to be "in a relationship" with you, then you know they are a true friend — and that you can trust them.

I have tried to keep these communication tips as brief and simple as possible — but this does not mean this little book is to be taken lightly. You hold a powerful tool in your hands that can help you improve all of your relationships — and, ultimately, improve the quality of your life and help you realize your goals and dreams.

INTRODUCTION

Communication is a huge part of our human experience — not only with others but within ourselves as well. While helping clients with their relationship problems, I often spend the majority of our sessions teaching them communication skills. These skills don't save every relationship, but most couples find that practicing these skills helps them get along with, appreciate, and understand each other better. In addition, this better communication brings greater clarity and greater understanding of themselves.

Being able to express ourselves effectively provides us with not only more choices but more opportunities to live as we choose.

Once two people learn to communicate, they can truly better understand each other. They may still disagree, but with better communication skills, they can understand why the other thinks and feels the way he or she does.

In the relationship groups I lead, I often ask heterosexual people what they are looking for in a mate, and they often reply that they are searching for someone like themselves. So, I ask, if they are looking for someone *like* themselves, why then are they seeking out someone of the *opposite sex*? As it usually turns out, most people want to be with someone who is different from themselves — so different, in fact, that they are opposites.

Most people actually desire the chemistry or friction that happens between two opposites, but they also want to enjoy and appreciate their differences rather than suffer as a result of them. The joy in relationships comes when we are able to celebrate our differences, and communication is the key to understanding, relating to, and celebrating those differences.

Despite the many books available on relationships and communication, the divorce rate in most

English-speaking countries still hovers somewhere around fifty percent. Obviously, a lot of couples still have difficulties relating to and communicating with each other. Many of the couples I interview say they have neither the time nor the desire to sit down and study an entire book on relationships.

This thirty-minute guide presents twenty basic communication tips that can be practiced at your own pace. Every person and every relationship is somewhat unique, so feel free to adjust the wording of these tips to your own style of speaking and understanding. All these skills are easy to learn, but it takes practice to remember them in day-to-day living.

WITH PRACTICE, CHORES BECOME HABITS, AND HABITS BECOME JOYS.

TIP 1

PUT YOUR
FRIENDSHIP FIRST—
EVEN BEFORE YOUR
LOVE RELATIONSHIP.

Friends usually put each other first, while those who have become lovers without developing a true friendship often put themselves or the relationship first. Often, people get so involved in their relationship that they forget to care about their mate as an individual. They are so concerned about getting what they want or need that they no longer care about their partner's needs. They play the game of love, with their lover as their opponent. They compete to get their own needs met, believing that if they do, the relationship will work.

Those who put their friendship with each other first can create fulfilling relationships. This doesn't mean putting your partner's needs as an individual before your own; it does mean putting your partner's needs as an individual before the needs of the relationship. Friends not only love each other, but genuinely like and accept one another just as they are. Lovers, on the other hand, often want to change or improve each other to fit their own needs.

Couples that are true friends stay friends even if they split up. They acknowledge they can't be a couple, but they still care about and enjoy each other's company. They want each other to be in a fulfilling relationship. Those who were just lovers can be possessive and jealous of their ex-partner's new love and happiness.

When you have a friendship, instead of going to your other friends for help or advice about what you should do in your relationship, you and your mate can work together as friends, turning to each other for advice about what you should do in your relationship.

For example, if you and a good friend are working together on a project and have a disagreement about it, you wouldn't let that disagreement come between you. Instead, you would work together as a team to find a solution — the problem is outside of your friendship and can't affect it.

Don't let your relationship as lovers put a wedge

between the two of you as friends.

THE FIRE OF TRUE FRIENDSHIP
REMAINS LONG AFTER THE
SPARK OF ROMANTIC LOVE.

TIP 2

DON'T BRING UP IMPORTANT
ISSUES DURING RUSHED
OR STRESSFUL TIMES
OF THE DAY.

It is a good practice to voice feelings as soon as they occur; however, if you have an emotionally charged issue to discuss, it is best to wait until you both have the time to sit and talk things through. Bringing up issues during inopportune times can be perceived as nagging. Don't nag! It only irritates.

Avoid emotional issues when you are tired and during stressful or rushed times, such as before work, right after work, or during any other period or in any location where you won't have enough time or privacy to give your full attention and fully discuss the issue.

Before talking to your partner, ask whether he or she is in a listening or talking mood. If your partner is not, try to set a better time when you will both be in the mood for discussion.

If you find that you and your partner have any past issues that you haven't dealt with, then you most likely have some damaging feelings such as resentment, anger, or defensiveness stored up. These dark feelings are guaranteed to continue to under-mine your relationship, and will not go away until you choose to deal with them. Your first priority must be to find working solutions for every one of those issues, solutions that both of you feel good about, without any trace of hard feelings such as anger or resentment.

As problems arise between the two of you, either discuss and resolve the problems as they arise, or make some form of temporary agreement until a permanent agreement can be reached. If you can't come up with a solution, then get professional help, but don't ignore the problem.

When you ignore a problem, negative feelings tend to increase and eventually overshadow your positive feelings until, at some point, you look back and recognize only a long, overwhelming list of what *doesn't* work between you. All too often this results in the end of a relationship that might otherwise have worked if problems had been dealt with as they arose.

UNRESOLVED PROBLEMS GROW
AND ARE FERTILIZED BY TIME.

TIP 3

DON'T CONFRONT YOUR MATE WITH A "PRE-SET" JUDGMENT THAT HE OR SHE IS WRONG OR AT FAULT.

If you confront your partner because you think he or she is wrong or at fault, and you happen to be mistaken, then you both are going to bear the extra burden of overcoming your pre-set judgment in order for the truth to be known.

Even if there is only a small chance that you're wrong about your partner being at fault, it will be harder for the truth to be seen if your opinions are already set. Also, putting your partner on the defensive is not conducive to smooth, open communication.

Instead, when you see or feel a problem, initiate the conversation with "I" statements.

Some examples of "I" statements are:

"I don't understand this situation."
"I need your help to figure this out."
"I have a problem with what you said."

These are ways of putting any initial blame on

yourself — thus helping your partner to be less defensive and more willing to work on the problem.

USE YOUR MATE AS A SOUNDING
BOARD, NOT A DART BOARD!

TIP 4

FIRST KNOW WHAT YOU <u>DO</u> WANT.

Often people "nag" about what they don't like or don't want, and yet they fail to tell their mate what they do want. Before you confront your partner with a complaint, get as clear as possible about what you *do* want in the situation — and *specifically* what you want from your partner. This way, if you get what you ask for, you can acknowledge it fully, drop the subject, and move on to the next moment.

In the heat of an argument we often get so much momentum built up that we have a tendency to keep arguing, even though we got what we initially asked for or wanted. So, be clear ahead of time as to what you want to get from the conversation, and if you do get it, acknowledge your mate with appreciation and don't keep asking for more.

When talking to your mate, keep in mind whether you want your mate to advise you, to fix it, to help you work it out, or to just listen to you. Then, explain what you want from your partner — don't expect him or her to guess.

Often people start arguments because they are seeking attention, intimacy, or drama and passion. If this is your tendency, find other, more productive ways to connect with your mate.

DON'T USE ARGUMENTS AND DRAMA AS A MEANS TO CONNECT OR GET ATTENTION.

TIP 5

FOCUS FIRST
ON THE PERSON
WITH THE CONCERN.

When our partner accuses us of something, often we automatically want to explain our side of it — how we see it. Even though this seems like a reasonable response, it is actually a defense and often unnecessary and counterproductive. When your partner confronts you on an issue, keep your focus on *your partner* and *your partner's feelings*. Treat your defense as a separate issue.

Ask questions and get as clear as you can about what is really going on with your mate. Often you will find that the problem is not yours, and you both can completely resolve it without shifting the focus to talk about yourself or whether you are responsible for your mate's problem.

Defensiveness arises from insecurity, and distracts us from the real issue.

TIP 6

ADDRESS ONLY ONE ISSUE AT A TIME.

During an argument, people often take and defend a position at all costs. They have a need to be right, and to help support their argument, they bring up issues from past times when they thought the other was wrong. This only adds to the complexity of the disagreement and makes it harder to reach an agreement.

Unless your intentions are to sit down and list all your issues so you can deal with them one by one, it is best to stick to the present issue and resolve it first, before you bring up any other issues.

VALID POINTS WILL STAND
ON THEIR OWN.

TIP 7
SAY PRECISELY WHAT YOU MEAN.

We often use generalities when we speak. Although our statements are clear to us, listeners may interpret something quite different. If you want to make an important point, take the time to say precisely what you mean.

Try to be specific and try to frame your statements and questions in a way that doesn't imply pre-set judgment of your partner's feelings or actions. As an example, suppose your partner is unusually quiet, and you think it's because he or she is angry at you. It is far better to ask "Are you angry with me?" than to ask "What are you angry about?" Note the important difference between these two questions. The first question — "Are you angry with me?" — leaves room in your own mind for change, just in case you are mistaken about your partner's feelings. The second question — "What are you angry about?" — implies that you have already decided how your partner feels. Whether you are right or wrong, your partner will probably resent the question.

Another example of being more precise is learning to distinguish between "feeling words" and "non-feeling words." Feeling words describe emotions. Instead of saying, "I feel like you don't listen" — stop! *"Like you don't listen"* is not an emotion. You can't feel it. What you do feel is hurt, anger, joy, etc. You can truthfully say "I *think* you don't listen," but not "I *feel* you don't." Only use the word *feel* when you couple it with an emotional word: "I feel *angry* when I am accused."

Speaking more precisely is one way to develop the habit of thinking more precisely before speaking. This allows you to become clearer about what your thoughts and feelings are, and what you wish to say.

PRECISE SPEECH REQUIRES SPECIFIC
THOUGHT, WHICH GIVES US MORE
DISTINCTIONS, HENCE MORE CHOICES
AND MORE OPPORTUNITIES.

TIP 8
PRACTICE ACTIVE LISTENING.

Along with speaking more articulately, practice listening more attentively. Try to be aware of distinctions in your partner's speech. If your mate says "My first impression of you was that you were immature," listen precisely to what they say; do not jump to conclusions and get defensive. They did not say that they think you *are* immature, but that their first impression of you *was* that you *were* immature. There is an important distinction between these two statements.

If you are discussing an important issue, try parroting or repeating what you heard back to your partner. If you question the validity of the statement, then repeat it back to them verbatim, just to check what you heard. This may feel awkward or contrived at first, but with practice it can greatly help to keep communication clear.

Sometimes when people hear their own words spoken back to them, it helps them realize that what they said is not what they meant to say.

If, however, your mate seems clear about what they meant to say, then you can paraphrase, or repeat back to your partner in your own words what you heard them say. This way you both know you're clear on what has been communicated.

OFTEN ALL A PERSON WANTS
IS SIMPLY TO KNOW HE OR SHE HAS
BEEN HEARD OR UNDERSTOOD.

TIP 9

USE "I" INSTEAD OF "YOU" STATEMENTS.

One of the most common causes of arguments is the "Blame Game" — blaming others or situations for how we feel instead of taking responsibility for our own emotions. Remember, it's not the situation or another's words or actions that cause our pain or anger, it's the meanings and judgments that *we* assign to others' behavior that causes our pain. People *cannot cause* emotions in other people, but they can say or do things that trigger negative thoughts, which in turn cause these emotions. You may be late due to your partner's forgetfulness, for example, but the anger you feel is your own doing, not theirs. If you were a patient person or if you weren't stressed out, their tardiness wouldn't have triggered your anger in the first place.

Learn to recognize the internal causes of your emotions, accept responsibility for them, and then stop blaming others for how you feel. You can retrain your patterns of blame by learning to use "I" statements. "I" statements have three possible parts: They state what's happening, how you are feeling, and/or why you feel that way. Here's an example that includes all three parts: "When you are late, I feel angry *because I'm* too embarrassed to show up last."

In "I" statements, always follow the word *because* with the word *I*. If *because* is followed by the word *you*, then it becomes a blaming "you" statement: "When you are late, I feel angry because *you* are always inconsiderate." When your mate hears "you" statements, he or she may feel accused and become defensive. This makes communication more difficult.

"YOU" STATEMENTS	vs.	"I" STATEMENTS
"You upset me."		"I feel upset."
"You're always late."		"I don't like waiting."
"You're a slob."		"I don't like picking up after you."

NO ONE BUT YOURSELF
IS RESPONSIBLE FOR
HOW YOU FEEL.

TIP 10

MAKE REQUESTS, NOT DEMANDS.

A true request asks for something with the understanding that any answer, including refusal, will be acceptable. A demand asks for something, expecting it to be given.

A demand is usually easy to recognize, because if you don't grant it, you'll be punished in some way. "Punishment" may take the form of a remark, a gesture, or even a subtle reaction, like silence or just turning away.

Our lives become much easier when we are

able to make requests of those we love, rather than demands.

True requests obligate no one.

TIP 11

REPLY TO, RATHER THAN REACT TO, YOUR PARTNER.

Because "reacting" is such a common cause of miscommunication and misunderstanding, this is one of the most important tips in this book.

Reacting is nonverbal; it is an indirect attempt to *show* someone how you think or feel. On the other hand, "replying" means verbalizing or stating directly to your partner your thoughts and feelings. Reacting is doing something in response to what your partner says or does, instead of simply talking to them about it.

When you react or change the course of your actions because of something your partner says or does, you are no longer living your life according to your own design. Instead, you are letting another's words or actions control, or at least influence, your behavior.

If your partner does or says something that causes you to create feelings you don't approve of and you, in turn, judge yourself as being wrong for having those feelings, you may try to keep those feelings hidden. What always comes out, in one way or another, is your reaction. Your mate won't know what, if anything, they did wrong, so they end up playing a guessing game, trying to guess why you are behaving the way you are. If they guess wrong or react, rather than asking you directly what's going on, then you both end up guessing. All this guessing causes miscommunication, and it becomes even more difficult to understand each other.

Instead of automatically reacting to what your

mate said or did, first talk to them about it and decide if your reactions are appropriate.

WHEN YOU REACT TO YOUR MATE
AND THEY REACT TO YOUR
REACTION, YOU BOTH LOSE TOUCH
WITH YOUR INITIAL INTENTIONS.

TIP 12

EMOTIONS are NeVeR
WRONG — IT IS HOW YOU
REACT TO THEM
THAT CAUSES CONFLICT.

We often hesitate to talk to our partner because we don't like what we're feeling or because we think we're wrong for having those feelings.

Remember, though, that emotions are neither right nor wrong — they just are. It is usually how we choose to react or respond to them that creates conflict.

We often feel emotions we don't have words for. This can be confusing. Having a larger "emotional vocabulary" helps us make more distinctions and define our emotions better, which in turn offers more choices and more opportunities for effective communication. Remember, emotions don't judge.

One example of expanding your emotional vocabulary is to look beneath what you think is anger. You may find all sorts of feelings that might be better described as fear or hurt.

Usually our emotions are triggered by our thoughts, our interpretations, our judgments, or our memories. The difficult part about identifying emotions is that they can occur in combination, in varying degrees simultaneously, or even in opposition. A classic example takes place when a loved one comes home very late. It is possible to feel relieved, angry, and hurt, all at the same time.

We can dramatically improve our relationships when we accept our partner's feelings as natural, without judging them for having those feelings.

TO FEEL IS HUMAN. JUDGE YOUR REACTIONS RATHER THAN YOUR EMOTIONS.

TIP 13

PRACTICE EMPATHY.

When people nag or repeat the same statement over and over, it may be because they think they haven't been heard, or that a particular issue has been left unresolved. When people communicate their feelings, it is often a cry for empathy — they want to be validated; they want their feelings to be recognized and accepted. They don't always need you to agree with them or to understand *why* they feel the way they do. But they do need to know that you understand *how* they feel. When your partner asks for attention, they don't always want you to fix the situation. They may just want you to understand and acknowledge what they are feeling. For you to really hear their story may be all that is needed from you.

When your partner tells you their reasons for feeling the way they do, try just to listen without being defensive in any way. If an angry child screams "I hate you," adults usually feel more concern about how the child feels than about their own hurt feelings. Give the same unconditional empathy to your partner.

BEING COMPASSIONATE MEANS
EMPATHIZING WITH SOMEONE, NOT
NECESSARILY UNDERSTANDING THEM.

TIP 14

MAKE AN EFFORT TO HEAR THE "PLEASE" BEHIND YOUR MATE'S WORDS.

All communication consists of three types of messages: relaying information, saying "please," or saying "thank you." Even if your partner is yelling at you, they're wanting something — they're saying "Please try to hear me" or "Try to understand that in some way I am hurting."

Instead of getting defensive about what your mate is saying, try *pleasing* your mate — try to hear the "please" behind their words. Pleasing is hearing the inarticulate speech of the heart. Consider what your partner is really asking for, but for some reason is unable to express at that moment. After all, which is more important, understanding the *need* behind your partner's words, or proving you are right once again?

UNDERNEATH EVERY ARGUMENT IS A
FRUSTRATED DESIRE FOR SOMETHING —
FIND OUT WHAT IT IS.

TIP 15

TELL YOUR MATE YOUR FEELINGS AS SOON AS YOU REALIZE YOU FEEL THEM.

In movies you may notice that almost every relationship problem occurs because of a lack of clear communication. Problems always seem to happen because one person believes something about the other that isn't true. It is better to chance being a fool — and risk rejection — by saying how you feel or by asking whether what you suspect is true, than to continue acting on false assumptions. Once again, don't hold back!

There is an exception to this rule, however:

Sometimes an incident will trigger a repressed emotion. We think we feel that emotion because of what triggered it. Usually you can identify repressed feelings because they are stronger than the situation warrants. In these instances, it may be best to wait and identify the source of the repressed feelings before you "dump" on your mate.

For example, you might snap at your partner for leaving the house at night without telling you, but the real reason for your upset stems from finding yourself unexpectedly alone, which triggered old memories of being abandoned earlier in life.

NO PERSON OR SITUATION CAN MAKE YOU ANGRY — THOUGH THEY MAY TRIGGER ANGER THAT YOU HAVE STORED INSIDE YOU.

TIP 16

BE 100% HONEST, 100% OF THE TIME.

Well, 99.99 percent of the time. Telling your partner that he or she looks ugly today usually doesn't help communication, but learning to be artfully direct can help.

If your partner knows you're telling them everything — the dirt as well as the good things — then they are more likely to trust you, because they know you are being honest with them, and therefore they don't have to constantly guess what you are thinking or feeling.

If you are wondering something about your mate, ask them about it. Ask about everything you want to know. If there are any topics the two of you can't talk about, it may eventually undermine the trust you have for each other.

Some years ago, I conducted a survey of couples that had been married more than fifty years. The primary element most couples claimed kept them together for so many years was trust. Trust is developed by feeling safe, and you feel safe when you are able to be truly honest with someone.

Communication and relationship skills are learned, and often take a lot of practice. On the other hand, being honest is something everyone can do, in spite of age or experience.

I often hear people say that even though they were confused, upset, or had many unhealthy emotional problems in their relationship, they still take pride in the fact that they have always been honest with their mate.

YOU NEED HONESTY TO HAVE TRUST,
TRUST TO HAVE FRIENDSHIP,
AND FRIENDSHIP TO ENJOY
A LASTING RELATIONSHIP.

TIP 17

MAINTAIN A SENSE OF LIGHTNESS AND HUMOR.

People have a tendency to get heated during discussions and forget they're talking to someone they love. Just because you are both discussing an important topic doesn't mean you have to take yourselves so seriously. People who have lived together successfully for years have learned that it is easier to deal with important matters if they keep the mood light and maintain a sense of humor, even during an argument.

Some friends of mine, for example, got into an

argument that built into this exchange:

Pat: "If you don't change, I'm leaving."

Chris: "Me, too — can I come with you?"

They both laughed, and their humor helped dissolve their defensiveness.

YOUR SENSE OF HUMOR REFLECTS YOUR
OUTLOOK ON LIFE AND YOUR ATTITUDE
TOWARD YOUR RELATIONSHIP.

TIP 18

DON'T BE A MIND-READER.

The better you know someone, the better you can understand or "read" them. Even if your mate says nothing to you, you often have an idea of how they feel and *why* they feel the way they do.

When communicating about important issues, however, assuming you know what the other is thinking or why they are doing what they are doing often leads to problems. And if you *act* on wrong assumptions, it can lead to even greater problems. If the topic is important, then it is important enough to discuss with your mate, to be sure you understand them correctly. Don't try to read their mind, and don't expect your partner to read your mind. If it is an important issue, tell them clearly what you want them to know. Don't expect your mate to understand your hints and reactions.

Sometimes when we suspect our mate of doing something wrong, we feel too embarrassed or ashamed to admit to them that we doubt them, especially if we fear that our suspicions could be wrong. So, we hint around or joke about it, probing for the truth, trying not to reveal our intentions to our mate until we get enough evidence to confront them about it. Instead of indirectly *alluding* to your suspicions, admit them; ask your mate what is really going on with them. Don't mind-read and then pry or hint, hoping that your mate will divulge the truth. Be direct.

IT IS BETTER TO ASK AND RISK EMBARRASSMENT THAN TO CONTINUE WITH FALSE ASSUMPTIONS.

TIP 19
KEEP THE
"PRIME DIRECTIVE."

Sometimes we need to say something to someone but we are afraid they may get hurt, angry, or take what we say the wrong way. In these instances, it's important that you first connect with them on a heart level, putting the love and feelings that you have for each other foremost. This is the *prime directive*, and it needs to take priority over all issues or positions that arise in your relationship.

When talking to someone about a difficult subject, expose your emotions to them; tell them first how you are feeling right then and there. Let them know how difficult the topic is for you. Reveal to them your fears or concerns about how they will react. Emphasize that you care about them and that you don't want to jeopardize or lose their friendship.

Some animals, such as horses and dogs, offer peace by exposing their neck, their most vulnerable spot, to their opponent. It is their way of saying, "Look, I have no desire to compete or fight with you; I am trusting you not to hurt me." When the other animal sees there is nothing to fear or defend, it usually stops the attack and lets its guard down.

It's the same with people you trust. If you open your heart to show them your vulnerability, your fears of being hurt or of hurting them, they will feel a desire — almost an obligation — to protect your feelings and to honor the trust you are extending toward them.

Keep communication with loved ones on a feeling level. Always assure them that their feelings are more important to you than any issues that may arise. If you confront your mate with an open heart, and keep the feelings of love you have for them up front and foremost, they may still react as you feared, but the connection and the reassurance that you care for them will help make what you say easier for them to hear.

NEVER LET ISSUES SEPARATE YOU
FROM THE FEELINGS THAT YOU
HAVE FOR YOUR PARTNER.

TIP 20

PRACTICE CLEAR COMMUNICATION.

Clear, direct communication honors each person's needs and feelings at all times. Here is a basic model that helps you clearly express yourself (an example follows at the bottom of page 95):

"When _____ happens, I feel _____ (an emotion) . . . because I want _____.

"What I imagine is that you _____. (*This is optional.*)

"What I would like from you now is _____.

"In the future, I would like for you to _____."

Here's the basic communication model for understanding your mate (an example follows on page 97):

"When _____ happens, how do you feel?

"What do you want instead?

"What would you like from me now?

"In the future, what would you like from me?"

Here are some examples of clear, direct communication in conversation.

When the conversation is focused on your needs:

"When the *radio wakes me up*, I feel *angry*

   . . . because I want *to sleep longer*.

"What I imagine is that you *aren't aware of how*

   loud the radio is in my bedroom." (*This is optional.*)

"What I would like from you now is *for you to*

   tell me if you understand why I am angry.

"In the future, I would like for you to *play the*

   radio softer when you know that I am home."

When the conversation is focused on your mate's

needs:

Dana: "When I *get upset and walk away*, how do you feel?"

Kim: "I feel *frustrated* because all communication stops."

Dana: "What would you like me to do instead?"

Kim: "I want you to stay and work through it with me."

Dana: "What would you like from me now?"

Kim: "For you to acknowledge that walking away isn't always the best way to handle things."

Dana: "In the future, what would you like from me?"

Kim: "I want you to initiate these conversations when you sense something is amiss."

Remember, clear, direct communicating:

- Is replying — *telling* — your partner how you feel or what you think instead of reacting to — or *showing* — your partner.
- Discusses feelings, not just thoughts.

- Uses "I" statements when focusing on yourself, rather than "you" statements.
- Does not blame anyone. You take responsibility for your own thoughts and feelings.
- Says specifically what you want now, or asks your partner specifically what he or she wants from you now.
- Consists of more than just telling your partner what you don't want or asking what he or she doesn't want.

- Makes requests, rather than demands.
- Clearly states what you or your partner want in the future.

THE THREE MOST IMPORTANT
FACTORS IN COMMUNICATION are
FEELINGS, FEELINGS, and FEELINGS.

AFTERWORD

Often my clients ask me how I can bear dealing with other people's problems all the time. They ask if it ever gets to me. My reply is that I enjoy it. I often give the analogy of how miserable it would be to hang onto the side of a thousand-foot cliff with no one to help you. Yet, some people travel all over the world just to be in that situation, purely for the joy and challenge of climbing. They enjoy it so much because they possess the skills and the tools necessary to help them make it to the top. It is the same with relationships and personal problems. When people have the tools and skills required to integrate changes and to initiate personal growth, they find it is a joy to get involved with self-help or relationship processes. They enjoy the challenge of acquiring, testing, and practicing with their new tools.

Although someone may theoretically know all

the skills and techniques required to climb a mountain, that person will never be a climber until he or she actually gets out and physically does it. The same applies to communication. Just knowing all these tips cannot make you a good communicator. Only using them can do that.

Hopefully, this book is a good introduction to those who haven't yet realized what great resources books can be for learning those tools that help relationships prosper. For those who have already read a lot about communication, this book may serve as an easy reference or quick reminder of tools they have already learned but need to practice.

Until someone is able to master these tips, the best communication advice I can give is to be honest and to just talk — and talk and talk. Talk about feelings, thoughts, suspicions, and questions. Even if you don't know how to say something correctly, talking enough will eventually reveal enough truth so that trust can be rekindled.

ABOUT THE AUTHOR

Doyle Barnett left the Ozarks as a teenager to join a Zen monastery. From there, he joined the Brotherhood of the Sun, an Eastern spiritual order founded by a disciple of the famous yogi Paramahansa Yogananda, where he lived and studied for nine years.

Now he is a certified master neuro-linguistic programmer (NLP) with the Society of NLP and the Advanced Training Institute. He is also a certified mediator by the Mediation Group, along with the Community Mediation Program of Santa Barbara County. He is a member of the Isla Vista Mediation program and the Southern California Mediation Association. Doyle also works as an advocate at the Santa Barbara Rape Crisis Center.

He has a private practice in the Santa Barbara area that includes NLP training for other professionals in the counseling field and for various human services organizations. He has led groups on relationships and communication since 1987.

His works have been published in various magazines, and he is a frequent guest speaker on radio and television.

For information about the groups he leads on communication, relationships, NLP training, mediation, or private sessions, contact:

Doyle Barnett
535 Barker Pass Road
Montecito, California 93108
(805) 969-3157
Fax: (805) 969-3157

ACKNOWLEDGMENT

Tips 10, 14, and 20 were inspired by the work of Dr. Marshall B. Rosenberg, founder of the Center for Nonviolent Communication, Cleveland Heights, Ohio (used by permission).

NEW WORLD LIBRARY is dedicated to publishing books and cassettes that help improve the quality of our lives. If you enjoyed *20 Communication Tips for Couples*, we highly recommend the following books and cassettes:

Relationships as Mirrors audio cassette, by Shakti Gawain.

Recipes for Romance, by Leslie and Jimmy Caplan.

Tantra for the West: Everyday Miracles and Other Steps for Transformation, by Marc Allen.

For a catalog of our complete library
of fine books and cassettes, contact:

New World Library
14 Pamaron Way
Novato, CA 94949

Phone: (415) 884-2100
Fax: (415) 884-2199
Or call toll free: (800) 972-6657
Catalog requests: Ext. 50
Ordering: Ext. 52

E-mail: escort@nwlib.com
www.newworldlibrary.com